SERVING YOUR COUNTRY

THE UNITED STATES AIR FORCE

by Michael Green

Content Consultant:

James Petersen
United States Air Force (retired)

CAPSTONE
HIGH/LOW BOOKS
an imprint of Capstone Press

CAPSTONE PRESS

818 North Willow Street • Mankato, Minnesota 56001
http://www.capstone-press.com

Library of Congress Cataloging-in-Publication Data
Green, Michael, 1952-
    The United States Air Force/by Michael Green.
        p. cm. -- (Serving your country)
    Includes bibliographical references (p. 45) and index.
    Summary: An introduction to the history, function, aircraft, and future
of the United States Air Force.
    ISBN 1-56065-687-5
    1. United States. Air Force--Juvenile literature. [1. United States.
Air Force.] I. Title. II. Series.
UG633.G76 1998
358.4'1'0973--dc21

                                       97-40063
                                         CIP
                                           AC

Editorial credits:
Editor, Matt Doeden; cover design, Timothy Halldin; illustrations,
   James Franklin; photo research, Michelle L. Norstad
Photo credits:
U.S. Air Force, cover, 4, 15, 22, 24, 26, 29, 30, 32, 38, 40, 43
American Airpower Heritage Museum, 12
Archive Photos, 10
Department of Defense, 16, 18, 20
International Stock/G. E. Pakenham, 37
Unicorn Stock Photos/Aneal Vohra, 8, 34

Table of Contents

Chapter 1
The U.S. Air Force

The United States Air Force is one of the armed forces of the U.S. military. The air force uses aircraft to defend the nation. The air force also builds and tests new airplanes and weapons.

Some members of the air force are pilots. But most people in the air force do not fly aircraft. These people do all the things that keep the air force working. They fix aircraft. They design new aircraft. They watch to make sure enemies do not attack.

Officers and Airmen

The air force includes two main groups. One group is officers. The other group is enlisted

The U.S. Air Force is made up of officers and airmen.

members. Enlisted members are called airmen. Both men and women can be officers or airmen.

Officers have higher ranks than airmen. They have more training than airmen. Airmen have to obey the orders officers give them.

There are about 350,000 people in the air force. About 70,000 of them are officers. About 15,000 of these officers are pilots. All pilots are officers. The rest of the people in the air force are enlisted members or reserves. Reserves are members of the air force who do not work full time.

The highest-ranking air force officer is the chief of staff. The chief of staff is a general. General is the highest rank an officer can earn. The chief of staff runs the air force and makes sure it is ready for battle.

The Air Staff helps the chief of staff run the air force. The Air Staff is a group of generals that controls different parts of the U.S. Air Force. The Air Staff helps the chief of staff decide how to use the air force.

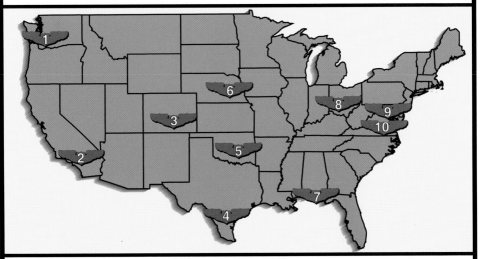

IMPORTANT U.S. AIR FORCE BASES

1) McChord Air Force Base, WA
2) Edwards Air Force Base, CA
3) U.S. Air Force Academy, CO
4) Lackland Air Force Base, TX
5) Tinker Air Force Base, OK
6) Offutt Air Force Base, NE
7) Eglin Air Force Base, FL
8) Wright-Patterson Air Force Base, OH
9) Bollings Air Force Base, D.C.
10) Langley Air Force Base, VA

Air Force Bases

Most officers and airmen work at air force bases. An air force base is like a small city. Many airmen and officers work together to defend the base and the United States.

Many air force members live in rooms or apartments on bases. Others live in houses near the bases.

Air force bases have many buildings where officers and airmen do their jobs. Some air force members work in offices on bases. Others work in hospitals or hangars. A hangar is a structure used to store aircraft.

Tours of Duty

Officers and airmen each serve at least one tour of duty. A tour of duty is a set amount of service time. Tours of duty usually last about four years.

Air force members can serve several tours of duty. Most members earn higher ranks as they serve more tours of duty. They gain more responsibility. They also earn more pay.

Some air force members work in offices on bases.

Chapter 2
History

The United States Air Force began in 1947. That was when the government decided to make the air force a separate part of the military. Before 1947, the air force was part of the U.S. Army. It started as the U.S. Army Air Service in 1907.

The Army Air Service did not have any airplanes in 1907. It bought its first airplane from Orville and Wilbur Wright in 1909. The Wright brothers were the first people to build and fly an airplane. The Wright Flyer was the name of the Army Air Service's first airplane.

The Army Air Service bought more airplanes. The airplanes were faster and sturdier than the Wright Flyer. Soon, pilots began using guns in their airplanes.

The Army Air Service bought its first airplane in 1909.

The Army Air Forces became the world's strongest air force during World War II.

The World Wars

World War I (1914-1918) was the first war that included airplanes. In 1917 and 1918, the U.S. Army Air Service helped defeat the German military. Pilots watched for enemy troops. They also attacked enemy airplanes. Pilots shot at each other in dog fights. A dog fight is a battle between two or more aircraft.

The U.S. Army Air Service became the Army Air Forces (AAF) during World War II (1939-1945). The AAF helped a group of countries called the Allied nations defeat the Axis powers. The Allied nations included the United States, Canada, the United Kingdom, France, and Russia. The Axis powers were Germany, Japan, and Italy.

The AAF became the strongest air force in the world during World War II. The army trained thousands of pilots and built more than 230,000 new airplanes.

After the World Wars

The AAF became a separate part of the U.S. military in 1947. The government called it the U.S. Air Force.

Later that year, an air force pilot named Charles Yeager flew an airplane faster than the speed of sound. The speed of sound is about 758 miles (1,220 kilometers) per hour. Yeager was the first pilot ever to reach that speed. Yeager flew a plane called the Bell X-1.

Air force pilots flew new, fast airplanes during the Korean War (1950-1953). One of the most successful airplanes was the F-86 Sabre. Air force F-86 pilots shot down 10 enemy airplanes for every F-86 that was lost.

The air force helped the other parts of the U.S. military during the Vietnam War (1965-1975). Pilots flew bombing and rescue missions. A mission is a military task. Air force aircraft also transported soldiers.

Some air force officers went into space during the 1960s and 1970s. These air force officers were astronauts. They piloted spacecraft to the moon.

The air force helped defeat the Iraqi military during the Gulf War (1991). Air force pilots bombed Iraqi targets on the ground. They also transported ground troops and supplies.

Air Force pilots bombed Iraqi tanks during the Gulf War.

Chapter 3
Air Force Jobs

There are many jobs in the air force. Each member of the air force performs a certain job. Everyone in the air force works together to keep the United States safe.

Pilots

Pilots fly air force aircraft. Some fly large bombers or airplanes that carry supplies. Others fly helicopters or fighter planes.

All air force pilots must be officers. They must train to fly aircraft. They learn about many kinds of aircraft. They learn how to use weapons and instruments. They also learn about safety. Air force pilots know what their aircraft can and cannot do. This makes them skilled fliers and keeps them safe.

Pilots fly air force aircraft.

Intelligence Officers

Air force intelligence officers gather information about other countries' air forces. They study new planes and weapons built by other countries. They help air force leaders know which kinds of weapons they will need to develop.

During wartime, many countries send messages in code. Some air force intelligence officers try to break these codes. Sometimes breaking codes helps the air force learn the enemies' plans.

Engine Mechanics

Air force engine mechanics keep aircraft engines working. They check airplane engines before and after flights. They look for and repair engine problems.

Air force engine mechanics test engines to make sure they will operate properly during flight. They test things like oil pressure and

Air force engine mechanics look for and repair engine problems.

Controllers use radar to help pilots fly aircraft.

temperature. They perform the tests to be sure pilots will be safe. Engine mechanics ground aircraft that have engine problems. Ground means to stop from flying.

Controllers

Air force controllers help pilots fly aircraft. Controllers work at air force bases. They decide which courses pilots will fly. They track where aircraft are and where they are going. Controllers also tell pilots what the weather will be like during their flights.

Air force controllers use radar to help pilots fly aircraft. Radar is machinery that uses radio waves to locate and guide objects. Controllers use radar to see if there are other aircraft nearby. They tell pilots when other aircraft come close.

Pararescuers

Some air force officers are pararescuers. Pararescuers try to help people whose aircraft have crashed. Pararescuers use parachutes to jump out of aircraft. A parachute is a large piece of strong, light cloth. Parachutes allow jumpers to float slowly and safely to the ground. Pararescuers jump into places where aircraft cannot land.

Pararescuers carry medical equipment. They know how to treat injured people. They may bring the people to places where aircraft can pick them up.

Chapter 4
Missions and Aircraft

Air force pilots fly different kinds of aircraft for different missions. Pilots fly bombers and fighters to attack enemies. They use transport planes to carry supplies to bases and mission sites. They use helicopters to carry and rescue ground troops.

Attack and Observation

The air force uses attack and observation aircraft to protect troops on the ground. Pilots flying these aircraft watch the sky and ground for enemies. Pilots use airplanes' weapons to defend troops if enemies appear.

The air force uses attack and observation aircraft like this A-10 to protect troops on the ground.

The A-10 Thunderbolt II is an attack and observation aircraft. The A-10 flies well at low speeds. This gives pilots time to watch the ground carefully. The A-10's weapons can destroy enemy aircraft and tanks.

Bombers

Bombers are the most important aircraft for attacking enemies. Bombers can fly long distances at high altitudes. Altitude is the height of an object above the ground. Bombers fly high so enemy weapons on the ground cannot hit them. Bombers drop bombs on enemy targets.

Some bombers are stealth aircraft. Stealth is the ability to fly quietly or secretly. Stealth aircraft have special kinds of engines. They also have special shapes. Radar cannot detect stealth aircraft. The B-2 Spirit is a stealth aircraft. B-2 pilots can fly bombing missions safely. Enemies may not even detect B-2s that are right over them.

The B-2 Spirit is a stealth aircraft.

Fighter planes like this F-16 carry powerful guns and missiles.

Not all bombers are stealth aircraft. Stealth aircraft are expensive to build. The B-52 Stratofortress is a large bomber that can fly at very high altitudes. It can also carry more bombs than other bombers.

Fighters

Fighters are important when the air force needs to defend a location. Fighters also fly with bombers to protect the bombers from enemy aircraft. Fighters are small and fast jet airplanes. They have powerful guns and missiles. A missile is an explosive that can fly long distances. Fighters can destroy enemy airplanes.

The F-16 Fighting Falcon is one of the best-known air force fighters. Another air force fighter is the F-15 Eagle. The F-15 is bigger and faster than the F-16. But it cannot turn or dive as quickly.

Helicopters

The air force uses helicopters to reach places where other aircraft cannot land. Helicopters do not need long air strips to land. An air strip is a smooth surface where airplanes take off and land.

The air force uses helicopters to rescue people who have become lost. It uses helicopters to reach people whose aircraft have crashed. Helicopters also carry troops into battles.

The air force uses the MH-60G Pave Hawk for search-and-rescue missions. It uses the HH-1H Iroquois to carry high-ranking officers into battles. The HH-1H also carries wounded soldiers.

Transport Aircraft

Transport aircraft carry supplies wherever the U.S. military needs them. Transport aircraft carry food, weapons, and people. Some carry trucks or tanks.

Some transport aircraft carry fuel. These aircraft can refuel fighters and bombers while still in the air. A transport aircraft that carries fuel is called a tanker.

The most famous air force transport aircraft is Air Force One. Air Force One carries the president of the United States. It also carries important members of the air force like the chief of staff.

Air Force One carries the president of the United States.

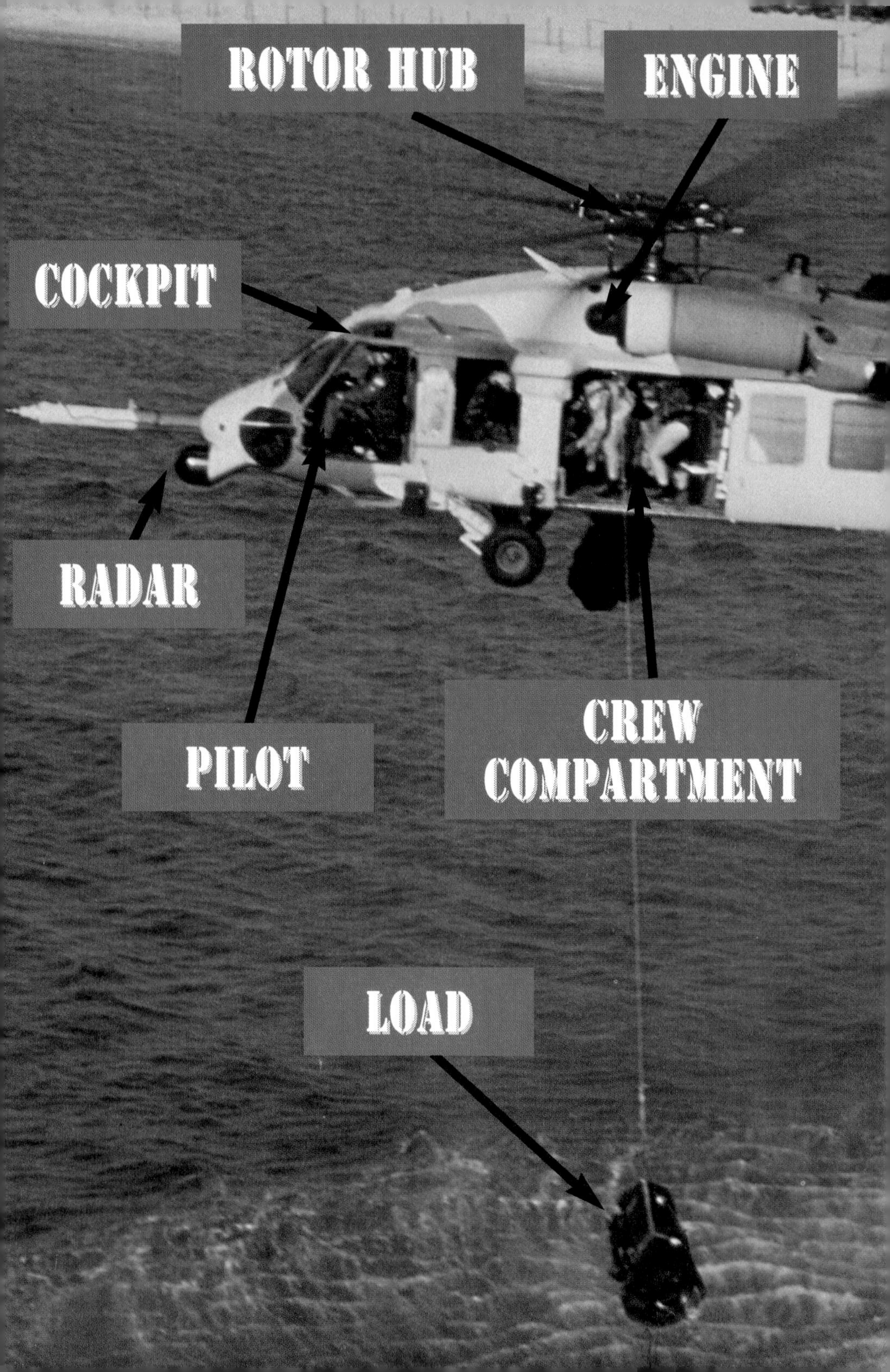

ROTOR HUB

ENGINE

COCKPIT

RADAR

PILOT

CREW COMPARTMENT

LOAD

TAIL ROTOR BLADES

TAIL WHEEL

MH-60G PAVE HAWK

Chapter 5
Training

Airmen and officers receive special training in the air force. They study in classes, take tests, and exercise. Members of the air force continue to train throughout their careers.

Airmen Training

Airmen begin their air force careers in basic training. Basic training is where airmen learn to be soldiers. Air force members in basic training are called airmen basic. Airmen basic are the lowest-ranking members of the air force.

Basic training lasts six weeks. Airmen basic learn about being in the air force. They exercise and take classes. They perform combat drills.

The air force promotes airmen basic when they finish basic training. Promote means to

---

Airmen and officers receive special training in the air force.

give someone a higher rank. The air force promotes airmen basic to the rank of airmen.

Most airmen go to duty stations after basic training. A duty station is where airmen work. Many duty stations are at air force bases. Airmen continue their training while they work at their duty stations. They learn how to do different air force jobs. They may earn higher ranks as they stay in the air force longer.

The highest rank an enlisted air force member can reach is chief master sergeant. Chief master sergeants work with both officers and airmen. They help airmen carry out officers' orders. They also tell officers when airmen have questions or complaints. Airmen usually serve about 20 years before they become chief master sergeants.

Officer Training

Air force officers receive special training that enlisted members do not receive. Officers may receive this training in three ways. They may

Airmen begin their air force careers in basic training.

train at the Air Force Academy, in an ROTC program, or at Officers Training School.

The Air Force Academy is located in Colorado Springs, Colorado. Cadets spend four years at the Air Force Academy. A cadet is someone training to be a military officer. Cadets learn about the air force and about different jobs. They go through drills and learn how to be leaders. They receive college degrees when they graduate. A degree is a title given to a person who has finished a course of study.

Some officers receive training through air force ROTC programs. An ROTC program teaches college students about leadership and the air force. Students at many colleges can enter ROTC programs.

College graduates can also become officers by completing Officers Training School. Officers Training School lasts three months. Members become officers when they graduate from the school.

Cadets go through drills at the Air Force Academy.

Air force officers start with the rank of second lieutenant. Second lieutenant is the lowest rank an officer can hold. The highest rank an officer can earn is general. There are four kinds of generals. They are brigadier, major, lieutenant, and full generals.

Air Force Reserves

Some officers and airmen join the Air Force Reserves. Reserve members are not on active duty. Active duty is full-time military work. Reserve members attend training on weekends once a month. They also train full-time for one or two weeks each year. The air force keeps its reserves in case it needs more people. The air force may place its reserves on active duty if there is a war.

Reserve officers and airmen go through the same training as active members. Many members of the reserves are people who have finished tours of duty. Others are people who work for the air force but also have other jobs.

The highest rank an officer can earn is general. This man is a lieutenant general.

Chapter 6
The Future

The U.S. Air Force is the most powerful air force in the world. The Soviet Union's air force was once as powerful as the U.S. Air Force. But the Soviet Union split into many countries in 1991. The air forces of these countries are not as powerful as the U.S. Air Force.

Many U.S. leaders now believe there is little chance of major wars. They believe there is no need for a large U.S. Air Force. The government has cut some of the air force's funding.

The air force continues to build new aircraft and weapons despite the funding cuts. New equipment helps the U.S. Air Force remain the most powerful air force in the world.

New equipment helps the U.S. Air Force stay powerful.

New Aircraft

The F-22 fighter is one of the new aircraft the air force is building. The air force wants the F-22 to replace the F-15 Eagle. The F-22 will be faster and harder for enemies to detect. It will have large guns and missiles. It will also have new computers that help pilots locate targets.

Another plane the air force is planning is the Joint Strike Fighter (JSF). The JSF will be fast and powerful like today's fighters. But the JSF will be cheaper to build than larger fighters like the F-22. The U.S. Navy and U.S. Marines will also use the JSF.

Future Defenses

Long-range missiles are one of the biggest threats to the United States. Long-range missiles can hit the United States from thousands of miles away. The air force is planning a special weapon system to destroy

The air force wants the F-22 to replace the F-15 Eagle.

long-range missiles. Airplanes will carry the weapon system. The airplanes will use lasers. A laser is a device that produces a narrow and powerful beam of light. Planes armed with lasers will be able to destroy enemy missiles.

WORDS TO KNOW

air strip (AIR STRIP)—a smooth surface where airplanes take off and land

altitude (AL-ti-tood)—the height of an object above the ground

general (JEN-ur-uhl)—the highest rank an officer can earn

mission (MISH-uhn)—a military task

parachute (PA-ruh-shoot)—a large piece of strong, light cloth; parachutes allow jumpers to float slowly and safely to the ground

promote (pruh-MOTE)—to give someone a higher rank

radar (RAY-dar)—machinery that uses radio waves to locate and guide objects

stealth (STELTH)—the ability to fly quietly or secretly

tanker (TANG-kur)—a transport aircraft that carries fuel

tour of duty (TOOR UV DOO-tee)—a set amount of service time

TO LEARN MORE

Blue, Rose. *The U.S. Air Force.* Brookfield, Conn.: Millbrook Press, 1993.

Hole, Dorothy. *The Air Force and You.* New York: Crestwood House, 1993.

Masters, Nancy Robinson. *Airplanes of World War II.* Mankato, Minn.: Capstone High/Low Books, 1998.

Schleifer, Jay. *Fighter Planes.* Minneapolis: Capstone Press, 1996.

USEFUL ADDRESSES

Air Force Historical Research Agency
Maxwell Air Force Base, AL 36112-5000

Air Force Public Affairs Resource Library
1600 Air Force Pentagon
Washington DC 20330-1690

Air Force Public Affairs Office
1690 Air Force Pentagon
Washington DC 20330-1690

Unites States Air Force Museum
Wright-Patterson Air Force Base
Dayton, OH 45433

San Diego Aerospace Museum
2001 Pan American Plaza
Bablo Park
San Diego, CA 92101

INTERNET SITES

United States Air Force Airbase
http://www.airforce.com/

National Air & Space Museum Homepage
http://www.nasm.edu/NASMpage.html

Air Force Kids Online
http://www.af.mil/aflinkjr/

Aircraft Images Archive
http://www.cs.ruu.nl/pub/AIRCRAFT-
  IMAGES/

INDEX